Editor
Sara Connolly

Editor in Chief
Karen J. Goldfluss, M.S. Ed.

Illustrator
Clint McKnight

Cover Artist
Diem Pascarella

Art Coordinator
Renée Mc Elwee

Imaging
James Edward Grace

Publisher

Mary D. Smith, M.S. Ed.

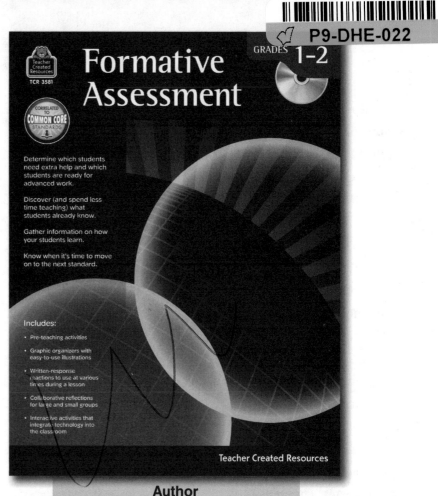

GRADES 1-2

Formative Assessment

Determine which students need extra help and which students are ready for advanced work.

Discover (and spend less time teaching) what students already know.

Gather information on how your students learn.

Know when it's time to move on to the next standard.

Includes:

- Pre-teaching activities
- Graphic organizers with easy-to-use illustrations
- Written-response reactions to use at various times during a lesson
- Collaborative reflections for large and small groups
- Interactive activities that integrate technology into the classroom

Teacher Created Resources

TCR 3581

Author

Susan Mackey Collins, M.Ed.

For correlations to Common Core State Standards, see page 5 or visit **http://www.teachercreated.com/standards/.**

Teacher Created Resources
6421 Industry Way
Westminster, CA 92683
www.teachercreated.com

ISBN: 978-1-4206-3581-2

© 2014 Teacher Created Resources
Made in U.S.A.

Teacher Created Resources

Table of Contents

Table of Contents *(cont.)*

Collaborative Reflections

Technology and Interactive Assessment

Introduction

Good assessment is vital to effective instruction. *Formative Assessment (Grades 1–2)* provides clear and effective resources to use for classroom formative assessments. Instructors in all subject areas must vary their methods of assessment to be sure each student clearly understands the standards being taught. This is where successful formative assessment is a must in any discipline.

Formative assessment provides feedback on a student's understanding of the concept being taught. The root word "form" in "formative" reminds the educator that the assessment method should be used to help *form* the lesson or skill being taught; the formative assessment can help the teacher decide if a student needs more instruction with a specific standard or has mastered the skill being taught and is ready to move on to something new.

Assessment that is formative should be used daily and provide classroom practice over the standard being taught. Methods of assessment can and should vary to ensure the teacher is meeting the differentiated learning styles of all students. Teachers should use formative assessment to ensure all students are successful with a specific standard before students are given a summative or graded assessment. Using formative assessment daily can also provide evidence that some students in the classroom are ready to move on to more advanced work with a specific standard. The results of formative assessment allow those students who are skilled in a specific area to be able to continue their own individual progress rather than waiting for other students to reach a specific goal.

This book is divided into five sections for quick and easy reference:

- **Pre-teaching:** formative assessment activities to use before a lesson

- **Graphic Organizers:** formative assessment organizers with easy-to-use illustrations

- **Written Response:** formative assessment reactions to use during various times during the lesson

- **Collaborative Reflections:** formative assessment activities to use with both small and large groups

- **Technology and Interactive Assessment:** formative assessment activities that integrate technology into the classroom.

Formative assessment is a necessary tool to help student achievement improve in all subjects and at all levels of learning.

Common Core Standards and Formative Assessment

Formative Assessment (Grades 1–2) is designed to be a teaching tool that helps implement formative assessment while teaching Common Core standards. Formative assessment is a vital part of making sure students are successful with Common Core standards. Since the standards provide a clear map for teaching literacy skills in all content areas, it is vital that all content areas be prepared to use formative assessments.

No matter how well a standard is written, if a student is not mastering the standard, he or she will not be successful and able to move on to the next higher level of learning. Good formative assessment allows a teacher to know what needs to happen next in the classroom and to meet the diversity of learning styles of each individual student. Good formative assessment also allows the student to be proactive in knowing where his or her weakness or strengths are in a particular standard. Self-assessment is key to formative assessment.

Common Core State Standards

Each activity in this book meets one or more of the following Common Core State Standards © Copyright 2010. National Governors Association Center for Best Practices and Council of Chief State School Officers. All rights reserved. For more information about the Common Core State Standards, go to **http://www.corestandards.org** or **http://www.teachercreated.com/standards/**.

Reading: Foundational Skills Standards	
Phonological Awareness	
ELA.RF.1.2	Demonstrate understanding of spoken words, syllables, and sounds (phonemes).
Phonics and Word Recognition	
ELA.RF.2.3	Know and apply grade-level phonics and word analysis skills in decoding words.
Speaking & Listening Standards	
Comprehension and Collaboration	
ELA.SL.1.1	Participate in collaborative conversations with diverse partners about grade 1 topics and texts with peers and adults in small and larger groups.
ELA.SL.1.2	Ask and answer questions about key details in a text read aloud or information presented orally or through other media.
ELA.SL.1.3	Ask and answer questions about what a speaker says in order to gather additional information or clarify something that is not understood.
ELA.SL.2.1	Participate in collaborative conversations with diverse partners about grade 2 topics and texts with peers and adults in small and larger groups.
ELA.SL.2.2	Recount or describe key ideas or details from a text read aloud or information presented orally or through other media.
ELA.SL.2.3	Ask and answer questions about what a speaker says in order to clarify comprehension, gather additional information, or deepen understanding of a topic or issue.
Presentation of Knowledge and Ideas	
ELA.SL.1.4	Describe people, places, things, and events with relevant details, expressing ideas and feelings clearly.
ELA.SL.1.5	Add drawings or other visual displays to descriptions when appropriate to clarify ideas, thoughts, and feelings.
Writing Standards	
Text Types and Purposes	
ELA.W.1.2	Write informative/explanatory texts in which they name a topic, supply some facts about the topic, and provide some sense of closure.
ELA.W.1.3	Write narratives in which they recount two or more appropriately sequenced events, include some details regarding what happened, use temporal words to signal event order, and provide some sense of closure.
ELA.W.2.2	Write informative/explanatory texts in which they introduce a topic, use facts and definitions to develop points, and provide a concluding statement or section.
Production and Distribution of Writing	
ELA.W.1.6	With guidance and support from adults, use a variety of digital tools to produce and publish writing, including in collaboration with peers.
ELA.W.2.6	With guidance and support from adults, use a variety of digital tools to produce and publish writing, including in collaboration with peers.
Research to Build and Present Knowledge	
ELA.W.2.8	Recall information from experiences or gather information from provided sources to answer a question.

Eight Great Ways to Use Formative Assessment

Use pre-assessment formative activities before beginning a unit. Assess where your class is as a whole. Use this information to decide where to begin and to see who might need extra help and who might be ready for advanced work.

Use pre-assessment formative activities to discover students who might need instruction outside the time in the regular classroom. Find time to meet with these students before starting a new unit or send home enrichment activities the student can do at home to help prepare him or her for the new standard.

Use the formative assessment activities to help form your lesson plans. Do not spend time teaching what your students already know; use the formative assessment activities to help you see which standards need the most focus.

Use formative assessment as rewards. Create incentive charts for students and give stickers to students who do well on the assessments. Have an agreed upon reward as individual students complete their charts.

Use formative assessment to gather information about your students. Find out how much your students remember from a previous year or even a previous unit to help you plan your lessons.

Use formative assessment for participation grades, not completion grades. Formative assessments show the teacher what a student knows at a certain point in the lesson; summative assessments show what a student knows at the end of the instruction.

Use formative assessment to gather information about the various learning styles of the students in the classroom. Use the information to help create differentiated instruction so that all the students can be successful while still adding rigor to the lesson.

Use formative assessment to know when it is time to give a summative or graded assessment. Mastery of formative assessments gives the teacher a clear understanding of when to move to the next standard.

Puppy Power

Use the activity on page 8 to pre-assess each student.

Find out what students already know about a standard **before** beginning the lesson.

Materials:

crayons, pencil, scissors, glue, and one copy for each student of page 8

Directions:

1. Make copies of page 8 for each student.
2. Explain to the students what they will be studying, but do not teach the lesson. For example, you might state that today the class will be learning about the different senses, but not explain what the individual senses are. Write the topic where all students can see.
3. Tell the students they are going to do an activity about today's lesson. Point out to the students that the topic is written on the board.
4. Pass out the worksheet and the materials needed to complete the activity. Explain to the class the directions they will need to follow to complete the activity.
   - Color the puppy's house, the puppy's dish, and the puppy on page 8.
   - Have an adult help you cut out the five bones at the bottom of the page.
   - On each dog bone, write or draw about the topic being studied, telling what you already know about it. (For the sample topic of the different senses, students might draw an eye or write words like "smell" or "hear.")
5. Tell students it is okay to leave a dog bone blank if they do not know any information. Encourage them to not feel discouraged if all or some of the bones are blank.
6. Have students glue all the dog bones on the dish, even if the bones are blank.

Something extra: Have students complete the bones after the lesson is taught or add new bones to the dish.

Name: _____

Puppy Power (cont.)

Directions:

1. Color this page.

2. Cut out the bones. Ask an adult if you need help cutting them out.

3. Write or draw on the bones what you know about today's lesson. If you don't know five things about this topic, you can leave some of the bones blank

4. Glue all the bones on the puppy's dish.

I Think; I Know

Directions: Explain to the students what topic they will be learning about in class. Write the topic where all students can see. State the topic and have students repeat the topic.

Make copies of the bottom section of this page for each student. Read and explain the directions to the class. Have students complete each section. If the student cannot write anything about the topic, have him or her draw a question mark on the lines provided.

Name: _____

Part 1

Directions: Write today's topic on the line.

Today's Topic: _____

Write two facts you know about this topic. Draw a **?** in each square if you do not know a fact.

1. ☐ _____

   _____

2. ☐ _____

   _____

After the lesson: Draw a smiley face in the square if the fact you wrote was true. Draw a picture on the back of this page about something you learned today.

Name: _____

I Know This

Listen as the teacher reads and explains the directions below.

1. Fill in the blank: Today we are going to study and learn about _____

    _____.

2. In the space below, draw a picture that shows what you already know about today's lesson. If you do not know what to draw, wait until the end of the lesson and then draw your picture.

Name: _____

Thinking "Ahead"

Directions: Listen carefully as the teacher reads each statement. Write your answer on the lines.

1. Today we will learn about _____.

2. What are your feelings about this topic? Circle your answer.

3. How much information do you already know about this topic? Circle your answer.

     A lot   Some   None

4. Why might someone need to learn about this topic?

   _____

   _____

   _____

   _____

   _____

Everybody Writes

Directions: Write the topic or standard that will be taught in a place where all the children can see. State the topic and have the students repeat it. Explain to the students they will be studying this topic; however, before the lesson begins, you want to ask what everyone might already know about it. Before you begin today's assessment, provide an example of what you want the students to do.

Tell the class that in a few minutes they will write or draw on the board what they already know about today's topic. Each student will have at least one chance to write on the board. Explain to the class you will first show an example.

For the example, write a sample topic on the board. An example that can be used is the joint topic "characters and setting." Tell students they will come up to the board a few at a time and write or draw something they know about the topic. Use the list below to show examples of what you might expect for the topic. Write the following words and phrases around the topic. Draw examples.

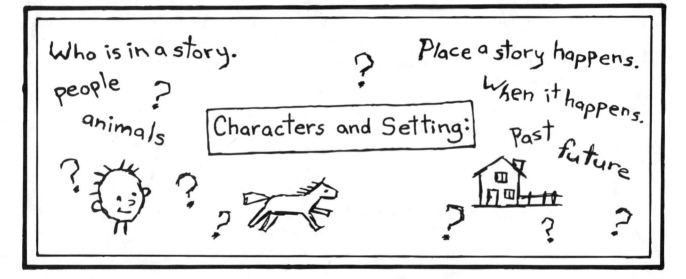

When you are finished, explain why these items might have been used. *Hint:* Be sure to do this with today's assessment, too.

Explanations: Characters are "who is in a story." Animals can be characters. Place is part of the setting. A story can take place "in the past." The picture represents a character. The question mark is written when a student cannot think of an idea.

Once the students understand what they will be doing, go back to today's lesson topic. State the topic again and have students repeat the topic. Allow five to ten minutes to complete the pre-assessment.

Name: _____

You Know So Much!

Formative Assessment

Listen carefully as the teacher reads the directions and tells the class what the topic of today's lesson is going to be. Use this information to complete the worksheet.

Directions: Think about what you already know about today's topic. Draw or write what you already know inside the book below.

I Know Lots of Things!

Name: _____

ABCs of Learning

Listen carefully as the teacher explains what the class will be learning about today. Complete the chart on page 15 after the teacher reads the directions to the class.

Directions:

Today's Topic: <u>Write the topic on the line.</u>

For the letter A—Draw "a" picture that has something to do with today's topic.

For the letter B—Write what you think the topic might "be" about today.

For the Letter C—Write about a place, other than school, where you might "see" the topic.

Example:

Today's Topic: <u>Shapes</u>

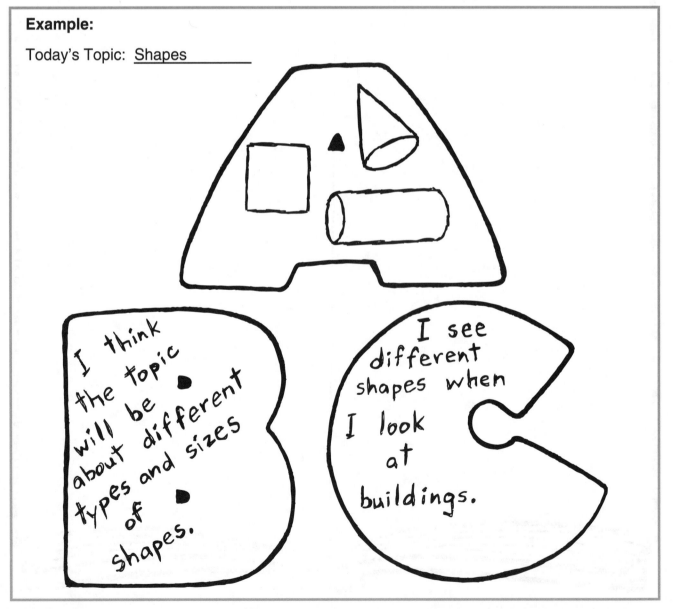

Name: _____

ABCs of Learning (cont.)

Today's Topic: _____

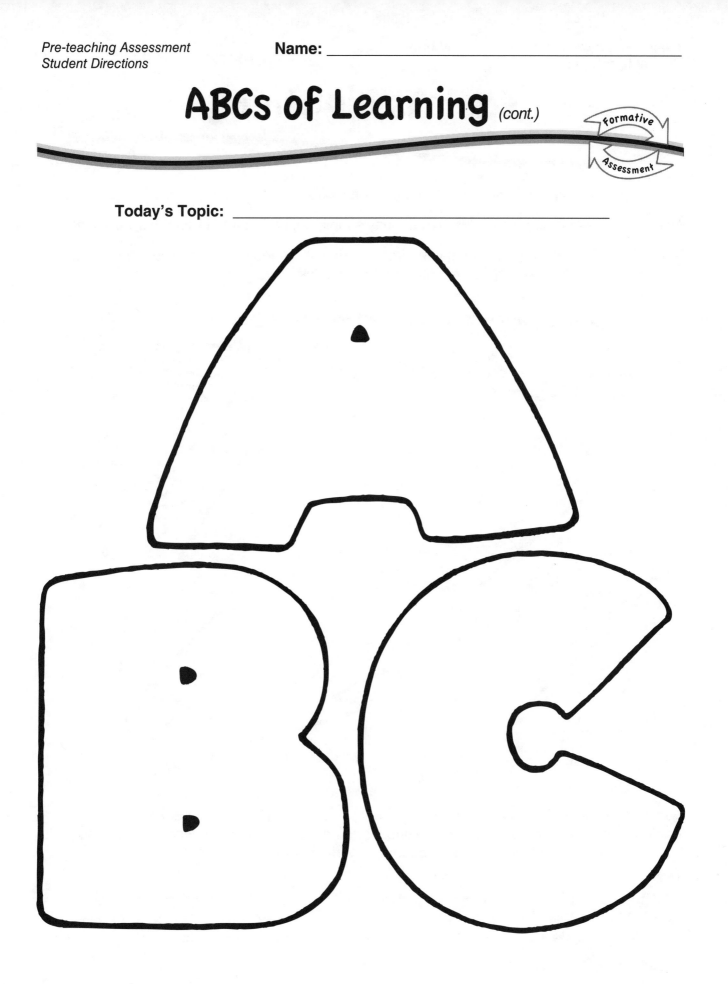

Name: _____

Fast As Lightning

Listen carefully as the teacher reads the directions.

Wait for the teacher to tell the class what today's topic will be before starting this worksheet.

Directions: Write or draw anything you already know about today's topic inside the bolt of lightning. You will have only five minutes, so be as quick as you can!

Something extra: When there is lightning, there is often thunder. Thunder can be very loud. Think about today's lesson. If you could shout and be loud like thunder, what is one thing that you would shout about what you learned today? Write your answer below.

Name: _____

Moon and Stars

Listen carefully as the teacher reads the directions to the class.

Directions: Inside the star, write one new word you learned in today's lesson. Inside the moon, write what the word means.

Something extra: On the back of this page, write a sentence using the new word.

Name: _____

Chalk Talk

Listen carefully as the teacher reads the directions to the class.

Directions: With your teacher's help, write the topic of today's lesson in the chalkboard. At the end of the lesson, write three things you learned on the lines on the chalk.

Name: _____

How Much?

Listen carefully as the teacher reads the directions to the class. You will need a crayon or colored pencil of any color.

Directions: Choose the column of stars that best shows how well you understood today's lesson. Color all the stars in the column you choose. Color column 1 if you understood the lesson very well. Color column 2 if you understood some, but not all of the lesson. Color column 3 if you did not understand any of the lesson.

Hint: Be ready to explain to the teacher why you chose column 1, 2, or 3.

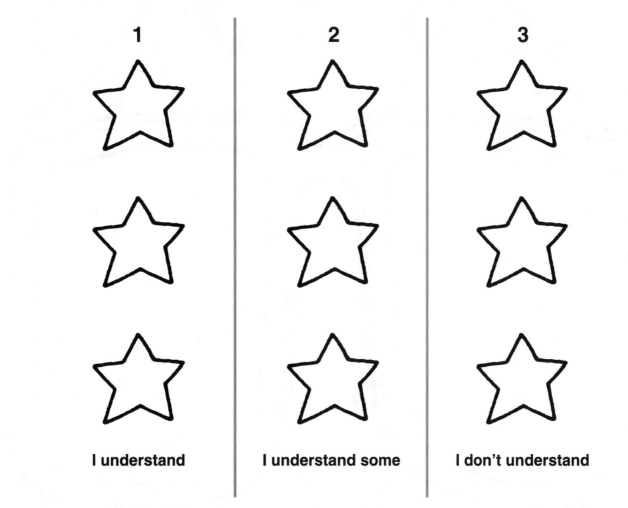

Something extra: If someone wanted to learn more about today's lesson, where could he or she look to find more information?

Name: _____

Look and Learn

Listen carefully as the teacher reads the directions to the class.

Directions: Think about what you saw in today's lesson. In one lens of the glasses, draw a picture of what you saw. In the other lens of the glasses, explain what you have drawn.

Something extra: On the back of this page, write a sentence explaining why today's lesson is important to learn.

Name: _____

Organize My Thoughts

Formative Assessment

Listen carefully as the teacher reads the directions to the class.

Directions:

During the lesson: Write key words you hear on the pots of gold beside each leprechaun. Some pots may remain blank.

After the lesson: Write what you would like to learn more about inside the shamrocks. Some shamrocks may remain blank.

How would you rate today's lesson? Choose a crayon and color the coins to rate the lesson.

Hint: 5 coins is the highest rating.

Something extra: On the back of this page, draw your own pot of gold with large coins. Write the topic of today's lesson on the pot. Draw pictures on your coins to show things you learned.

Name: _____

Compare and Contrast

Listen carefully as the teacher reads the directions to the class.

Directions: Follow each step.

    a. Write the topic of today's lesson on computer screen 1.

    b. Think of another topic you have studied in class. Write this on computer screen 2.

    c. Compare the two topics. Write two ways the topics are alike on screen 1.

    d. Contrast the two topics. Write two ways the topics are different on screen 2.

Name: _____

Fill It In

Formative
Assessment

Listen carefully as the teacher reads the directions to the class.

Directions: Complete each part of the worksheet to show what you know about the lesson.

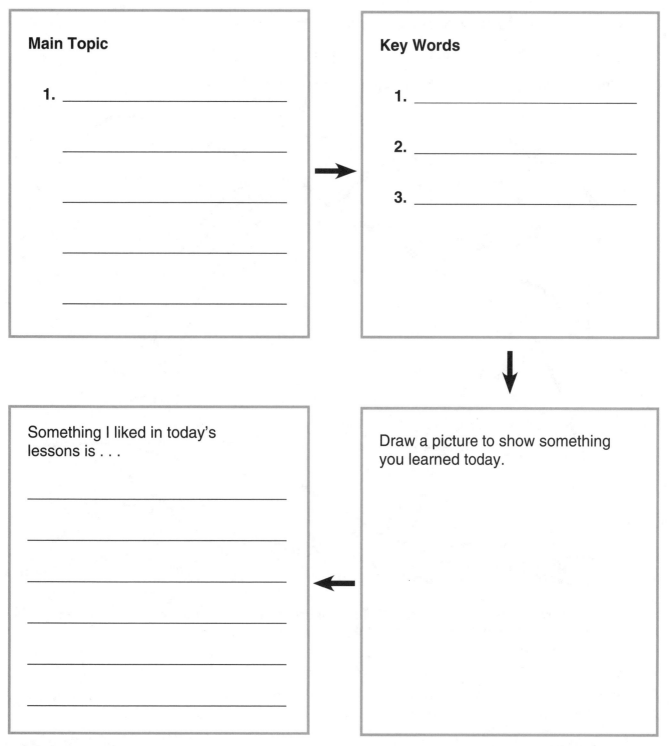

Main Topic

1. _____

_____

_____

_____

_____

Key Words

1. _____

2. _____

3. _____

Something I liked in today's lessons is . . .

_____

_____

_____

_____

_____

Draw a picture to show something you learned today.

Name: _____

Looking Sharp

Listen carefully as the teacher reads the directions to the class.

Directions: Follow each step.

   a. Write the topic of today's lesson on the pencil point.

   b. Write something you learned today on the pencil.

   c. Write a question you have about today's lesson on the eraser.

Something extra: There are many types of jobs in the world. Think about a job where today's lesson might be needed. Write the type of job on the line below.

_____

On the back of this page, draw a picture of a person working at the job you wrote. Be ready to explain why the person would use today's skill.

Name: _____

Key Ideas

Listen carefully as the teacher reads the directions to the class.

Directions: Think about what you learned today. Write three important, or "key", things you learned on the lines.

Something extra: Think of one key way you could use today's lesson outside of school. Write about or draw your idea on the back of this page.

Name: _____

Pin Board

Formative Assessment

Listen carefully as the teacher reads the directions to the class.

Directions: Write or draw an answer for each card. Each answer should be about today's lesson.

Name: _____

In and Out

Formative Assessment

Listen carefully as the teacher reads the directions to the class.

Directions: Write today's topic on the line below.

Before the lesson: Write two things you know about the topic on the paper in the "In" basket. If you cannot think of anything to write, draw a question mark on the paper.

After the lesson: Write two things you have learned about the topic on the paper in the "Out" basket.

Topic: _____

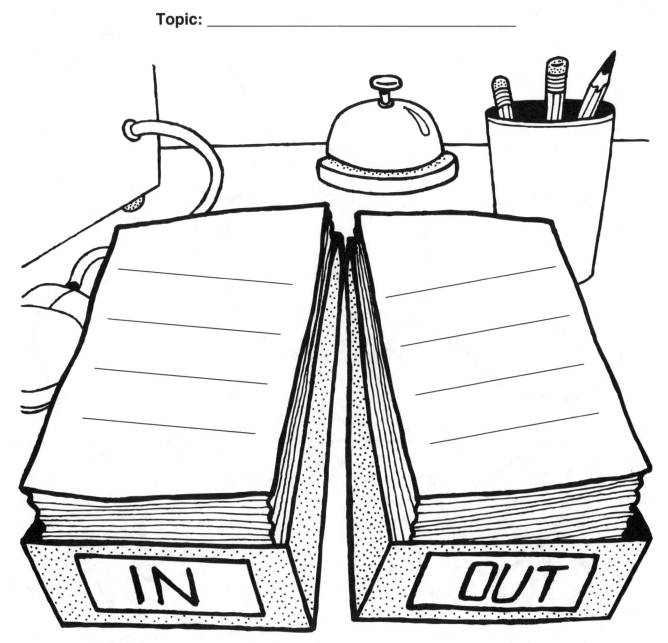

Name: _____

I Know This; I Know This Not

Listen carefully as the teacher reads the directions to the class.

Directions: Write today's topic in the center of the flower. Write or draw what you have learned on the petals of the flower.

Do you want to know more about something from today's lesson? Write your question at the bottom of the page.

My question:

_____

_____

Name: _____

The Number Three

Formative Assessment

Listen carefully as the teacher reads the directions to the class.

Directions: Three is an important number. In stories there are "three" little pigs or "three" bears, and people often get "three" wishes.

Think about the number three. Which three things in today's lesson do you think were the most important to learn?

Use the spaces below to write about the three most important things you learned today.

1

2

3

Name: _____

Tic-Tac-Toe, What Do You Know?

Formative Assessment

Teacher Directions: Make one copy of the student section of the worksheet at the bottom of the page. Then complete the copy of the tic-tac-toe board at the bottom of the page. Write out the topic of the lesson in the center square. Complete the remaining spaces with information, illustrations, or key words you want the students to learn by the end of the lesson. Make copies of the completed board and pass out the copies to each student near the end of the lesson. Read each section out loud to the class. Students will be instructed to draw a circle around concepts they feel they have mastered. Students will be instructed to draw an "X" on concepts they feel they do not understand.

****

Student Directions: Listen carefully as the teacher explains how to complete the tic-tac-toe board.

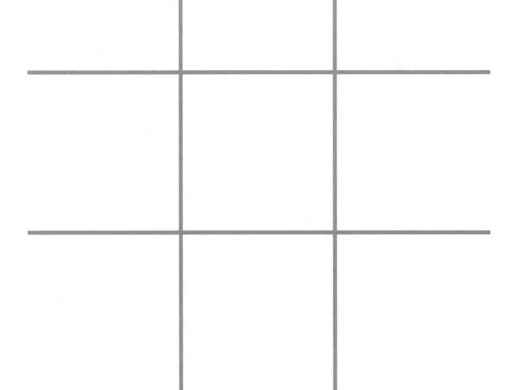

Name: _____

Power Up!

Formative Assessment

Listen carefully as the teacher reads the directions to the class. You will need one yellow crayon, one orange crayon, and one blue crayon.

Directions: Help give this rocket lots of word power! On the three parts of the rocket, write three key words you heard in today's lesson.

Use the color guide to complete the rocket:

Color the part yellow if you can tell your teacher what the word means.

Color the part orange if you need help remembering what the word means.

Color the part blue if you left the section blank.

Name: _____

Learning Magic

Listen carefully as the teacher reads the directions to the class. You will need one purple crayon and one orange crayon.

Directions: Complete each step as the teacher slowly and clearly reads each one.

Step 1: Write the topic of today's lesson on the magician's hat.

Step 2: Write a key word you learned on rabbit #1.

Step 3: Draw a picture that shows something you learned on rabbit #2.

Step 4: Color rabbit #3 purple if you understood today's lesson very well. Color rabbit #3 orange if you wish the teacher would explain the lesson more.

Topic

Name: _____

How Things Are Alike

Listen carefully as the teacher reads the directions to the class.

Directions: When you compare two things, you find ways the two things are alike, or similar.

Use the pear below to compare today's lesson to something else you already know about, or a topic given to you by the teacher.

List three ways the two topics are alike.

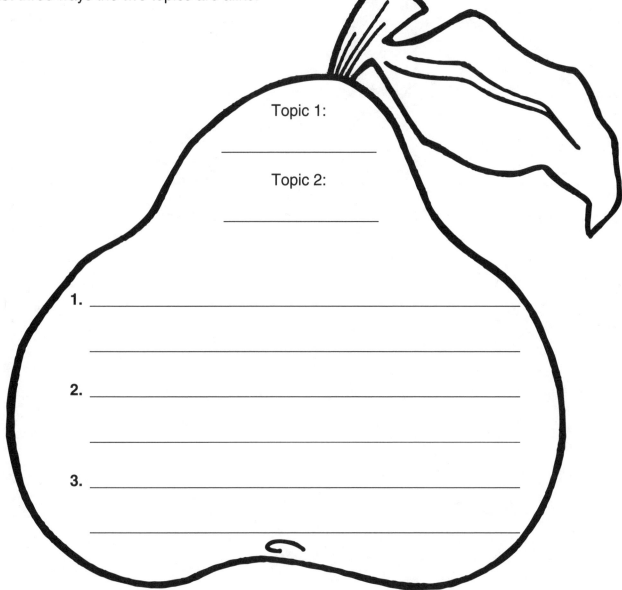

Topic 1:

_____

Topic 2:

_____

1. _____

_____

2. _____

_____

3. _____

_____

Something extra: On the back of this page, contrast the two topics. Write three ways the two topics are different.

Name: _____

Three Facts in a Row

Formative Assessment

Listen carefully as the teacher reads the directions to the class.

Directions: Think about three things you learned in today's lesson. Choose any three spaces in a row. Then write or draw the three things in the open spaces so that you have three facts in a row. Rows can be made up and down, side to side, or corner to corner.

Something extra: Is there anything about today's lesson that you still don't understand? Draw a large square on the back of this page and write your question in the center.

Name: _____

Write, Draw, Ask

Formative Assessment

Listen carefully as the teacher reads the directions to the class.

Directions: Read each direction and complete each part.

Draw what you learned about today.	Write two things you learned about today.
	1. _____ _____ _____ 2. _____ _____ _____
	Write a question you still have about today's lesson here. Draw a smiley face here if you do not have any questions. _____ _____ _____

Name: _____

Nuts About It

Formative
Assessment

Listen carefully as the teacher reads the directions to the class. You will need one purple crayon and one green crayon.

Directions: Complete each part.

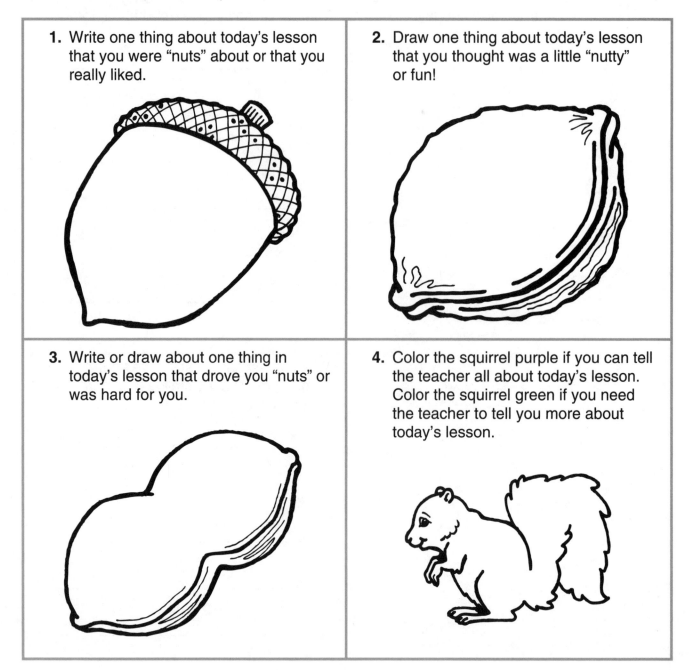

1. Write one thing about today's lesson that you were "nuts" about or that you really liked.

2. Draw one thing about today's lesson that you thought was a little "nutty" or fun!

3. Write or draw about one thing in today's lesson that drove you "nuts" or was hard for you.

4. Color the squirrel purple if you can tell the teacher all about today's lesson. Color the squirrel green if you need the teacher to tell you more about today's lesson.

Name: _____

Ducks in a Row

Formative Assessment

Understanding a Lesson with Steps

Think about the steps you learned in today's lesson. Then listen carefully as the teacher reads the directions to the class. You will need scissors, glue, one sheet of construction paper, a pencil, and one copy of the worksheet on page 38.

Directions: Use the worksheet on page 38 to complete the steps below.

Step 1: Cut out the ducks.

Step 2: Write today's topic on one of the ducks.

Step 3: Imagine you had to explain today's lesson to someone else. Write out the steps of the lesson. Write only one step on each duck. Use examples or write out the steps.

Step 4: Start with step one and put the ducks in the correct order. Glue the ducks in a row onto the construction paper.

Hint: You may not need to use all of the ducks.

Example:

Name: _____

Ducks in a Row (cont.)

Name: _____

Super Hero

Listen carefully as the teacher reads the directions to the class.

Part 1

Directions: Write two things you thought were super about today's lesson on the hero's cape.

Part 2

Directions: For every superhero, there is a villain who makes things hard. What one thing about today's lesson was hard for you?

_____

Something extra: On the back of this page, draw and color a picture of a villain to go with today's superhero.

Name: _____

Where Could I Learn More?

Formative Assessment

Listen carefully as the teacher reads the directions to the class.

Directions: Write a question you have about today's lesson. If you do not have any questions, draw a smiley face on the lines.

_____

_____

_____

_____

If you wanted to learn more about today's lesson, which source would be the best to use? Circle the answer. You can circle more than one.

Something extra: On the back of this page, draw a picture of another source that you could use to get more information about today's lesson.

Name: _____

Just Three Steps

Formative Assessment

Directions: Listen carefully as the teacher reads the worksheet to the class. Answer each part as it is read to you.

1. Today in class we studied this topic:

Write or draw your answer.

2. This is an example the teacher showed us in class:

3. Here is an example of my own that shows what we studied in class:

Name: _____

I Remember

Formative Assessment

Listen carefully as the teacher reads the directions to the class.

Directions: If you reflect on something, you think about it or you imagine it happening again. For example, if you had a wonderful birthday party, a few days later you might reflect on all the fun things you did at the party.

Use the space below to reflect on today's lesson. Write about three things that you most remember.

1. _____

_____

_____

2. _____

_____

_____

3. _____

_____

_____

Name: _____

Apples for the Teacher

Listen carefully as the teacher reads the directions to the class. You will need one green crayon, one yellow crayon, and one red crayon.

Directions: Give your teacher some very special apples by finishing this page. Complete each part of this sheet as the directions are read to you.

1. Color this apple **red** if you understood today's lesson very well.

Color this apple **yellow** if you understood some of today's lesson but not all of it.

Color this apple **green** if you did not understand today's lesson and would like more help.

2. Write an important word you heard during the lesson.

3. Write a definition for the word you wrote inside apple #2.

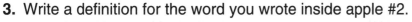

Name: _____

Write and Draw

Listen carefully as the teacher reads the directions to the class.

Part 1

Directions: Write two key words from today's lesson. Draw an illustration for each key word.

1. Key word: _____

Illustration:

2. Key word: _____

Illustration:

Part 2

Directions: Write a sentence with each key word.

1. _____

2. _____

Name: _____

Say It with a Poem

Formative Assessment

Listen carefully as the teacher reads the directions to the class.

Directions: Write a poem that tells what you learned from today's lesson. Use the back of this page if you need extra space.

Example:

What Makes a Shape?

We had lots of fun today,
We made shapes with sticks and clay.
A triangle has three sides to it,
The shape and color can change a bit.

Name: _____

Starting Slow and Steady

Listen carefully as the teacher reads the directions to the class.

Directions: Write four key words you hear during the lesson on the back of the turtle.

Something extra: Think fast! Use one of the key words in a sentence of your own.

_____

_____

Name: _____

One Thing

Listen carefully as the teacher reads the directions to the class.

Directions: Help the Thing Monster finish his work. Write an answer for each number. If you cannot think of an answer, write a question mark (?) on the line.

1. One thing I like about today's lesson is . . .

○ _____

_____

_____

_____

2. One thing I do not understand very well is . . .

_____

_____

○ _____

_____

3. One thing I can draw about today's lesson is . . .

○

Name: _____

Color, Then Write

Listen carefully as the teacher reads the directions to the class. You will need crayons or colored pencils.

Directions:

Step 1: Color the picture that best shows how you feel about today's lesson.

Step 2: Write a sentence explaining why you feel this way.

I feel this way about today's lesson because

_____

_____

I feel this way about today's lesson because

_____

_____

I feel this way about today's lesson because

_____

_____

I feel this way about today's lesson because

_____

_____

Name: _____

Dear Teacher

Formative Assessment

Listen carefully as the teacher reads the directions to the class.

Directions: Use the journal space to write a letter to your teacher. Write at least three sentences about today's lesson. The first sentence is started for you.

Dear Teacher,

Today we learned all about _____

_____

_____

_____

_____

_____

_____

Something extra: On the back of this page, write a note to a friend or someone in your family. Tell them something about today's lesson that you did not tell your teacher!

Name: _____

Short and Sweet

Formative Assessment

Listen carefully as the teacher reads the directions to the class. You will need crayons or colored pencils.

Directions: Show what you know about today's lesson by completing each step.

Step 1: Write at least two key words from today's lesson on the frosting.

Step 2: Write one question you have about today's lesson on the cupcake wrapper.

Step 3: Color sprinkles on your cupcake if you understand today's lesson. Color the frosting yellow if you need the teacher to explain more about today's lesson.

Name: _____

Grade Yourself

Listen carefully as the teacher reads the directions to the class.

Directions: Give yourself a grade on the report card by using the scale below. Draw a symbol in each square.

Grading Scale:  Yes   Maybe   No

My Report Card

Skill	Grade
I can tell the teacher what today's lesson was all about.	
I can give an example from today's lesson if I were asked.	
I still need to learn more about today's topic.	
I feel like I really understood today's topic.	

Something extra: On the back of this worksheet, write a sentence that summarizes or explains today's lesson.

Name: _____

The Four Ws

Listen carefully as the teacher reads the directions to the class.

Directions: Write an answer for each column.

Who or **What** is today's lesson about?	**When** could you use this skill?	**Where** might you use this skill?	**Why** do you need to learn this skill?

52

Name: _____

Everyone's Talking

Formative Assessment

Listen carefully as the teacher reads the directions to the class.

Directions: All of the students in the picture are talking about today's lesson. Write and/or draw what the students are telling each other about today's topic.

Everyone is talking about today's lesson: _____

today's topic

Something extra: Pretend you have a question about today's lesson. On the back of this page, draw a picture of you calling another student, and then write a question you might ask about the lesson.

Question: _____

Name: _____

Fishing Hooks

Listen carefully as the teacher reads the directions to the class.

Directions: Write an answer on a hook. Then, write a rhyming word on the fish to make a match.

Example: I know rhyming words share the same ending sound.

1. I know a key word from today's lesson.

2. I can give an example of what I learned in class.

3. I can write one word to tell how I felt about today's class.

4. I have one question I want to ask about today's lesson.

Name: _____

How I Feel

Listen carefully as the teacher reads the directions to the class.

Directions: Write an answer to complete each sentence.

Use the words from the box to help you answer each one.

sad	good	bad	happy	wonderful
amazing	sure	worried	upset	great
unsure	certain	amazing	calm	uncertain

1. I feel _____ about today's topic.

2. I feel _____ that I learned about this topic today.

3. I feel _____ that I could tell someone else about what I learned today.

4. I feel _____ that I could tell my teacher three facts about today's lesson.

5. I feel _____ when I learn something new.

Something extra: Show how you feel about today's lesson. Draw a picture that shows your feelings about what you learned today.

Name: _____

Celebrate

Formative Assessment

Listen carefully as the teacher reads the directions to the class. Work with a partner chosen for you by the teacher and celebrate how smart you are by writing the answers to each question. You will need crayons or colored pencils.

Directions: Work with a partner to find the answers to each question. Write the answers inside the balloons. Color each balloon that has an answer.

Hint: You can share answers with a partner, but each of you will write on your own page.

1. Today's lesson was all about . . .

2. Here is one example of what I learned today:

3. This would be a great question for a quiz about today's topic:

4. One word I could use to describe today's lesson is . . .

Name: _____

Talk a Little

Formative Assessment

Listen carefully as the teacher reads the directions to the class.

Directions:

1. Use the space below to write and draw as many things as you can about today's lesson.

2. Wait for your turn. The teacher will call on you for a short one-on-one talk about today's lesson.

3. Circle two things you would like to tell the teacher about today's lesson.

Name: _____

Guess

Listen carefully as the teacher reads the directions to the class. You will work with a partner the teacher has chosen for you to complete this worksheet.

Part 1

Directions: Draw a picture about today's lesson. When you are both done, swap papers to complete Part 2.

Part 2

Directions: Make sure you have your partner's paper. Look at the picture. Write two sentences about your partner's picture.

Hint: If you need help, ask your partner to tell you about the picture.

This picture is all about _____

_____

_____

_____

_____

Part 3

Directions: Look at your own paper. Read what your partner wrote. Is he or she right? Explain your picture to your partner.

Name: _____

Rhyme Time

Formative Assessment

Listen carefully as the teacher reads the directions to the class. Before you complete this page, wait for the teacher to divide the class into small groups of three to four students.

Directions: Work with the students in your group to complete each part. Each student must have answers written on his or her own page.

1. Write a key word you learned in today's lesson. Then write a word that rhymes or nearly rhymes with your new word.

> **Example:**
>
> light and bright (These words have the same ending sound. These two words rhyme.)
>
> carnivore and uniform (These two words nearly rhyme.)

_____ and _____

2. Write a short rhyme to tell about something you learned in class.

> **Example:** Carnivores eat only meat;
>
> Herbivores are what I'd rather greet.

_____

_____

_____

_____

3. Write a rhyme to a friend telling all about today's lesson.

_____

_____

_____

_____

4. Circle the rhyming word that best shows how your group feels about today's lesson.

Glad   Sad

Name: _____

Fact and Opinion

Formative Assessment

Listen carefully as the teacher reads the directions to the class. Before you complete this page, wait for the teacher to divide the class into small groups of three to four students.

Directions: Work with your partners to find the answers. Each student must have answers written on his or her own page.

1. Write one fact about today's lesson.

_____

_____

_____

2. Write one opinion about today's lesson.

_____

_____

_____

3. Give an example or draw a picture that illustrates a fact about today's lesson.

Up and Down

Part 1

Teacher Directions: Prepare a list of facts students should know about today's lesson. Make a copy of this page and use the space below to record the six facts.

1. _____

2. _____

3. _____

4. _____

5. _____

6. _____

Part 2

Teacher Directions: Prepare a list of statements that are not true about today's lesson. Write the four statements on the lines below.

1. _____

2. _____

3. _____

4. _____

Part 3

Teacher Directions: Explain to the class that you will be reading out loud ten different statements. Mix up the statements from Part 1 and Part 2 when reading them out loud.

Tell the students if a statement is true or a fact, the students will hold both arms straight up. Tell the students if a statement is false or not true, the students will put both arms straight down. Watch carefully as the students answer to see who is and who is not answering correctly. Use the information to help plan any further lessons about the topic.

Name: _____

I Say, You Say

Listen carefully as the teacher reads the directions to the class. The teacher will divide the class into groups of two or three students. Wait for the teacher's instructions to go on to a new part of the worksheet.

Part 1

Directions: Choose someone in the group to go first. The student going first will tell one fact about today's lesson. The next person will tell another fact about the lesson. Each person in the group will continue to tell facts about the lesson. The group is finished when no one can think of any more facts.

Part 2

Directions: Talk with everyone in the group. Decide which fact you learned today that is the most important. Each person writes the group's choice on his or her worksheet.

This is the most important thing we learned today:

_____

_____

_____

Part 3

Directions: Ask each person in the group why today's lesson is important. Write your answer below. How is this information important to you? Be prepared to explain your answer if your teacher calls on you.

_____

_____

_____

_____

_____

Name: _____

Report It

Formative Assessment

Listen carefully as the teacher reads the directions to the class.

Directions: Take this worksheet home. Pretend that a newspaper reporter is interviewing you. Ask someone at home to act as a reporter for your assignment and to record your spoken answers to the questions on the worksheet. Be sure to bring your worksheet back to class. Before you take this worksheet home, complete the line below with help from the teacher.

We studied _____ in class today.
         topic

Hint: If the person being interviewed does not know an answer, please draw a star on the line. Questions not answered are not marked wrong.

****

Today I am interviewing _____,
                                    student's name

1. What did you study today? _____

2. Tell me a key word you learned about this topic.

   Key word: _____

3. Why do you think this lesson was important for you to learn?

   _____

   _____

   _____

   _____

   _____

Face Me?

Directions: Make a copy of page 65. Have all students stand beside their desks. Students should be facing you. Explain to the class you will be asking them a list of true or false questions about today's lesson.

Explain if the student thinks the answer is true, he or she will face you. Explain if the student thinks the answer is false, he or she will turn and face away from you.

To help students remember which is the position for "true" and which is the position for "false," cut out the True and False cards on page 65 and tape them to the walls where students can see them.

Write the true and false statements on the lines below. *Hint:* Be sure to demonstrate how the students will answer before beginning the assessment.

True or False:

1. _____

    answer: _____

2. _____

    answer: _____

3. _____

    answer: _____

4. _____

    answer: _____

5. _____

    answer: _____

Be sure to use the back of this page if more space is needed for questions.

Something extra: Make extra copies of page 65 and have students hold up "True" and "False" cards to questions as an option for this activity.

Face Me? *(cont.)*

Directions: Cut out the True/False cards and use the instructions on page 64 to post cards in the classroom.

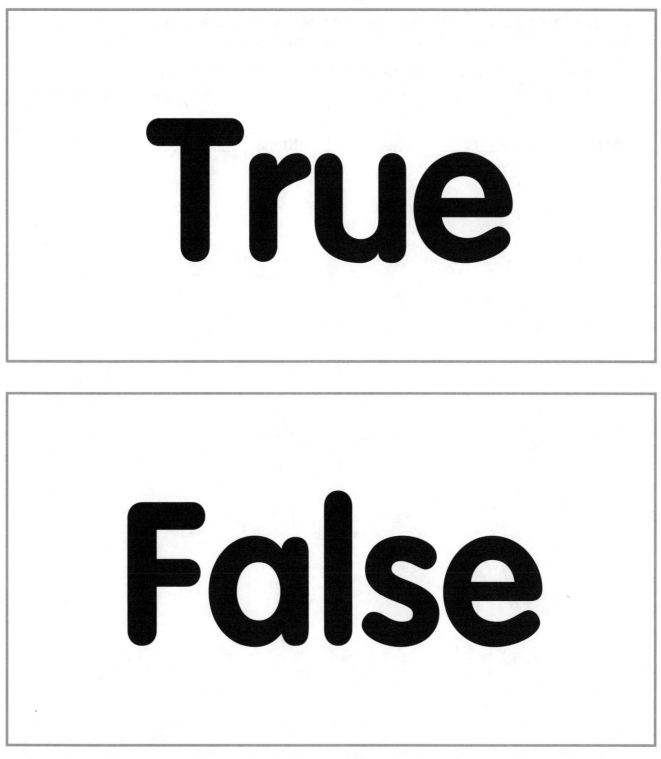

True

False

Name: _____

Find Four

formative
Assessment

Listen carefully as the teacher reads the directions to the class.

Directions: Write or draw something you learned about today's lesson in square 1.

Walk around the class and find three more students to write or draw three more facts about today's lesson. Have each student write his or her name and fact inside the square.

When you are finished, there should be four different examples on your page.

1. **Name:** _____	**2.** **Name:** _____
3. **Name:** _____	**4.** **Name:** _____

Right on Target

Listen carefully as the teacher reads the directions to the class. Before you complete this page, wait for the teacher to divide the class into small groups of three to four students.

Directions:

1. Write today's topic in the center or bull's-eye of the target.

2. With your group, write or draw something about today's lesson in the ring that touches the topic circle.

3. Write a question your group has about today's lesson in the outside ring.

Something extra: Draw an arrow in the box. Draw the arrow pointing *up* if you feel good about today's lesson. Draw the arrow pointing *right* if you feel okay about today's lesson. Draw the arrow pointing *down* if you feel like you need more help with today's lesson.

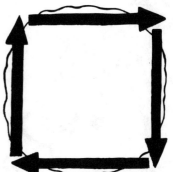

Name: _____

Draw, Don't Write

Listen carefully as the teacher reads the directions to the class. Before you complete this page, wait for the teacher to divide the class into groups of two or three students. You will need crayons or colored pencils and one worksheet for each group of students.

Directions: Work with your partners to complete the page. In the space below, draw and color pictures that explain or show something about today's lesson. Be ready to explain your picture(s) to the teacher.

Hint: Each person in the group should draw.

Name: _____

Keeping Track

Listen carefully as the teacher reads the directions to the class. Wait for the teacher to divide the class into small groups of three to four students to complete this page.

Directions: Move around the hurdles on the track by answering each question. Use the people in your group to help find the answers.

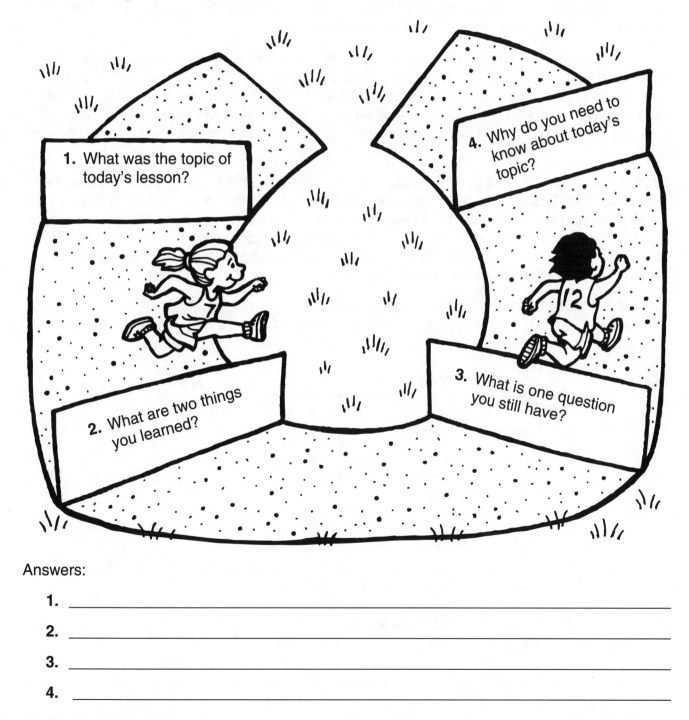

1. What was the topic of today's lesson?

2. What are two things you learned?

3. What is one question you still have?

4. Why do you need to know about today's topic?

Answers:

1. _____

2. _____

3. _____

4. _____

Group Sort

Materials: scissors, glue, one copy of page 71 (teacher-completed worksheet), and one copy of page 72 for each group

Directions: Make a copy of page 71. Write key terms, equations, definitions, or other information the students should know about today's lesson in the boxes on page 71. Add more strips if needed by making two copies of page 71. Include at least three terms or statements that are not true or that do not belong with today's lesson.

Divide students into small groups of three to four students. Give one copy of the completed page 71 to each group. Also give one copy of page 72 and a pair of scissors to each group. Students will cut out the boxes and work to sort the terms into two groups: **Yes** and **No**. **Yes** sorts are items that were important to the lesson or information taught during the lesson. **No** sorts are items that were not part of the lesson and are not pertinent to the material studied in class.

Explain to the students that any information that is correct or about today's lesson should be glued under the **Yes** column on the group's worksheet. Any information that is not true or does not belong should be glued onto page 72 under the **No** column on the group's worksheet. Monitor the groups and have each group explain the sorts and choices that were made. Take note of those students still having trouble with the activity and plan for more instruction and assessment for the topic with these children.

Something extra: Remove the items from the sort that were not about the lesson. Then have students sort into two columns using "Yes" as the column for items they feel they understand well, and using "No" as the column for items they feel they do not understand well.

Example:

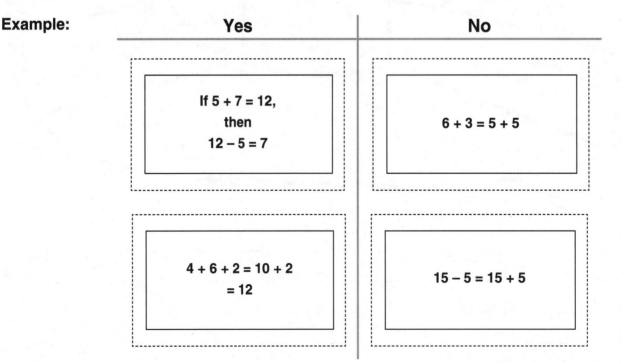

Yes	No
If 5 + 7 = 12, then 12 − 5 = 7	6 + 3 = 5 + 5
4 + 6 + 2 = 10 + 2 = 12	15 − 5 = 15 + 5

Name: _____

Group Sort *(cont.)*

Listen carefully as the teacher reads the directions to the class. Before you complete this page, wait for the teacher to divide the class into small groups of three to four students.

Directions: Each group will have one worksheet. Cut out each word box.

Use page 72 to finish the word sorts. Glue any rectangles that are important to today's lesson in the "Yes" column. Glue any rectangles that are not important to today's lesson in the "No" column.

Name: _____

Group Sort (cont.)

Yes	No

72

Name: _____

Ready to Pop

Listen carefully as the teacher reads the directions to the class. Before you complete this page, wait for the teacher to divide the class into small groups of three to four students. You will need scissors, glue, and one copy of page 74.

Directions: Talk to the other students in your group about today's lesson. Decide what are some of the most important things everyone learned.

Then write or draw six things you learned about today's lesson on the popcorn pieces on page 74. Cut out each piece and glue the pieces inside the popcorn bucket. *Hint:* Each person in a group can have the same answers.

Name: _____

Ready to Pop *(cont.)*

Listen carefully as the teacher reads the directions to the class. Before you complete this page, wait for the teacher to divide the class into small groups of three to four students.

Directions: Write or draw what you know about today's lesson on each piece of popcorn. Cut out the pieces and glue to the popcorn bucket on page 73. Be ready to tell the teacher which pieces of popcorn you completed.

Name: _____

First, Next, Finally

Formative
Assessment

Listen carefully as the teacher reads the directions to the class. Before you complete this page, wait for the teacher to divide the class into small groups of three to four students.

Directions: Work with your group to complete the worksheet. Everyone in the group must write or draw their answers on his or her own paper, but everyone in the group can have the same answers.

Today's lesson was all about _____

1. First, we learned . . .

2. Next, we learned . . .

3. Finally, we learned . . .

Something extra: On the back of this page, write or draw an answer to the following question:

Other than school, where or how can you use what you learned today?

Name: _____

Five-Minute Fact Find

Formative Assessment

Listen carefully as the teacher reads the directions to the class.

Part 1

Directions: You will have five minutes to finish Part 1. When the teacher gives the signal to begin, walk around the room with your paper and pencil and ask other students to write or draw on your paper something they learned today. *Hint:* If someone asks you, be sure to write and draw on other students' papers, too. Stop when the teacher gives the signal.

Part 2

Directions: On your paper, circle anything that is written or drawn that you know is true about the lesson. Do not circle the things you did not know or do not think are true.

Books Tell What You Know

formative
Assessment

Directions: Have students create short online books about any lesson. Students can work individually or in pairs to make their online creations.

Examples of websites: **www.storybird.com   www.storyjumper.com**

Students can add pictures with the touch of a button, but must type the content for each page. Be sure to give specific directions to get the results you want from the assessment.

Examples:

1. Explain the steps learned in today's lesson.

2. Summarize what you learned today.

3. Create a dictionary of key words and definitions about today's lesson.

4. Make a book of questions that you still have about today's lesson.

5. Answer these questions about today's lesson:

   who, what, when, where, and why?

6. Write a journal entry about what happened in class today.

7. Write a letter to someone you know and explain what you learned at school today.

8. Work with a partner and write a short book about today's lesson.

9. Write and explain how you can use what you learned today somewhere other than school.

10. Pretend you are a teacher. Write a story telling how you would explain today's lesson.

One-on-One

Directions: Before beginning this activity, make a copy of this page to document student assessment.

Next, use one-on-one time with students to assess what they have learned, while also creating a class visual for all the students to see.

Invite students to your desk, one at a time, to discuss a lesson you want to assess. Have students tell you in one to two sentences what the lesson was all about, or ask specific questions about key words or concepts. Have the remaining students at their desks engaged in a different activity while one-on-one assessments occur.

Type student responses into a word-processing document. Leave the responses that are typed anonymous. However, make notes in the section below about any student who has questions or seems unsure of the lesson. You can also use the list to keep track of students who have completed the one-on-one conference.

When all students have been assessed, show their responses to the class using an interactive whiteboard or any other mode available. Students will be able to see how their comments compared to those of their peers without feeling the pressure of answering out loud in a class discussion. Use this opportunity to discuss any parts of the lesson that a majority of the students had trouble with or point out any parts of the lesson that everyone mastered.

Formative Assessment Log Sheet

Student List

1. _____
2. _____
3. _____
4. _____
5. _____
6. _____
7. _____
8. _____
9. _____
10. _____

11. _____
12. _____
13. _____
14. _____
15. _____
16. _____
17. _____
18. _____
19. _____
20. _____

Wiggle Worms

Use a free music website or your own music to help complete this formative assessment.

Directions: Make a copy of the Wiggle Worms worksheet on page 80 for each student. Have students write or draw on the body of the wiggle worm five things that they learned during today's lesson.

Tell the students they are going to have the chance to become wiggle worms. Explain to the class you will be asking a series of questions. The questions will be true or false questions about the lesson. You will create the list of questions to be used at the bottom of this page.

Tell the students you will read the question to the class. You will repeat the question if needed. Once the question is read and everyone has heard the question, start the music. Each student will decide if the answer to the question is true or false. If the answer is true, the students will wiggle like wiggle worms as the music is playing. If the answer is false, the students will freeze like statues. Since students might not agree on the answers, it is possible some students will be "frozen" while others are "wiggling" to the music.

Stop the music and allow students to stop wiggling or unfreeze. Share the correct answer before moving on to the next question. Carefully observe which students are having difficulty answering any of the questions. Also look carefully at the work done by each student on page 80 to see which students fully understand the lesson.

True and False Questions (Use the back of this page if more space is needed.)

1. _____

   Answer: _____

2. _____

   Answer: _____

3. _____

   Answer: _____

4. _____

   Answer: _____

5. _____

   Answer: _____

6. _____

   Answer: _____

Name: _____

Wiggle Worms

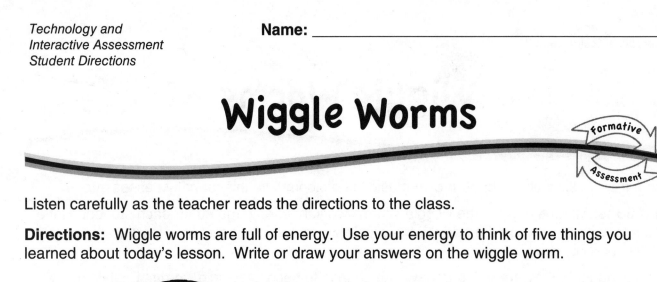

Listen carefully as the teacher reads the directions to the class.

Directions: Wiggle worms are full of energy. Use your energy to think of five things you learned about today's lesson. Write or draw your answers on the wiggle worm.